BIG BLISS
BLUEPRINT

100 LITTLE THOUGHTS
to build positive
LIFE CHANGES

SHELL PHELPS
M.A. Counseling Psychology, SHRM-CP

Positive Streak Publishing
P.O. Box 575
Pinckney, MI 48169

positivestreakpublishing@gmail.com

ISBN: 978-1-7345784-0-9 (print)
ISBN: 978-1-7345784-1-6 (ebook)

Ordering Information:

Special discounts are available on quantity purchases by corporations, associations, and others. For details, email phelpsstrategies@gmail.com, website: www.phelpsconsulting.net, or call us at (734) 845-2469

Dedication

If you're picking up this book, you're probably wondering who the dedication will be for. Well, this one is for you. Since you are seeing this book and reading this page, you dare to seek ways in which to improve your life. For that, I appreciate how hard it is to admit there is room for improvement, but proud you are ready for change. I'm dedicating this book to those in search of the potential of living a better life and wanting to find your happiness. Cheers to the start of creating your own big bliss!

If you are looking to schedule a personal strategy session, please visit our website at phelpsconsulting.net. By clicking on the Coaching page, you will see the available options, pricing, and appointment schedule. You will be able to book your own appointment right from the website.

If you are interested in obtaining a discount schedule for placing a bulk order of 10 or more copies of this book or to schedule a speaking engagement, please do not hesitate to call us at 734-845-2469 or email us at phelpsstrategies@gmail.com for the most current pricing.

If you like this book, please leave a review from the bookstore source you purchased it from. We would like to hear from you so please email us phelpsstrategies@gmail.com.

ACKNOWLEDGEMENTS

I would like to express my sincere gratitude to some very special people in my life who have supported this journey from the beginning to the end. To both my parents, Chuck and Cherie, who taught me the most about the School of Hard Knocks. I have since graduated due to their love and support. Those life lessons were monumental in forming these strategies.

Also, endless hugs and tribute to all three of my children, Amanda, Joe, and Xander, who have all contributed to this book in each of their own ways. I'm more than grateful for their love and unwavering encouragement. An extra special thank you to my grandchildren, closest friends, immediate family, and colleagues (who I now call friends) for their constant uplifting when those darn insecurities would sneak up on me. All these amazing people kept me moving forward. They know who they are!

Of course, to my devoted and die-hard #1 fan, my husband Paul, who taught me the true meaning of unconditional love. He believed in me and picked up the pieces in order for me to make my dream of sharing these strategies with those who desire to find their bliss so I could create a blueprint. Also, a huge heartfelt thank you to his parents for raising an incredibly kind, talented, and intelligent human being. Thank you for accepting me into your family as they have.

I couldn't have refined these strategies without my clients. To you, I hold our sessions most dear to my heart. All of you have taught me a wealth of knowledge just as much as I have hopefully helped you along the way. The sessions together were the most enlightening and continue to inspire my big bliss!

To T., who taught me at age 19 that life can be cut way too short so live your life now. I learned quickly to jump into life with both feet first. To everyone who is taking the time to read this book and trying to find your bliss, I hope you find it and continue to savor it. Thank you for reading!

CONTENTS

PREMISE

L ife is hard enough as it is; let's make it easier. If you're trying to be your best self and want to build on a solid foundation, you're in the right place. You can learn simplistic, positive ways to shift your focus in new directions at the right times to have better outcomes to life events.

- If you are not feeling content with your life, these strategies can give you a jump start. Changing your perspective is a great beginning to a happy ending.

- This book's style is easy to use. You can flip to any page or follow each themed section in order. It provides quick references for simple, thoughtful strategies to life's challenges when you get stuck or lost in the daily grind.

- Each page includes an easy-to-apply strategy that is designed to help you reflect, filter, and retrain your perspective on each topic to create change.

- At the end of each themed section, you will find reinforcement strategies to practice weekly. They are intended to support and enhance minor or major impacts by bringing it altogether.

- The strategies presented target thought-provoking remedies and ways to navigate life's situations when you're feeling unsure of how to move forward.

- These proactive methods can help you to continually propel forward by changing your automatic thought patterns one at a time for personal growth to have what and who you want in your life.

- It's not about being perfect but finding a balance in your life.

- The microscopic thoughts in this book will help you invest wisely and achieve a state of bliss. Let's take this journey together.

1

SMALL REFLECTIONS THAT PAY LOVING COMPOUND INTEREST

When we enter this world, our emotional bank accounts have very little available balance. The truth is, we are all dealt an unchangeable hand to start our lives. We don't get to choose who teaches us or how we are taught love. From the start, our caregivers teach us our first experience of love, giving us our first return on investment. This provides us with the fundamentals of giving and receiving unconditional love. We all deserve to be loved unconditionally. While some of us got lucky, others of us struggled with the quality of our caregivers.

When you were first shown love, it became your introduction to kindness. Being kind allows you the opportunity to share your life with someone else. Showing kindness is a gateway to inviting people into your heart. Loving words and actions are the way you make deposits into others' emotional accounts. The more deposits, the more interest you compound in your emotional savings account. When you reach that state of happiness, you give and receive love in abundant amounts.

UNCONDITIONAL LOVE IS A GIFT WITHOUT RESTRICTIONS

STRATEGY

Let down all barriers to truly love unconditionally. Give love as a gift to someone deserving, with a no-refund policy. Remove any "if" statements to love and replace with "because" statements. "If" statements are conditional; "because" statements are unconditional. Accept all aspects of the person, not just part of them. "I love this person because they make me feel alive again." Unconditional love is the best gift you can give someone, especially when you give it to yourself.

FLAWS AND ALL

STRATEGY

Accept all the different variations of being you; this includes the unperfected versions. This is truly a profound test. We all have good and not-so-good episodes in life. Own your flaws and defuse the critics. It's hard to debate with someone who agrees with you, and certainly more attractive when people acknowledge aspects of themselves that need work. It makes people more likeable and human.

Love the person you are now, not the person you aspire to be. Give yourself the opportunity to feel unconditional love for yourself. Discredit any shame in your game and be ok with you! Take the pressure off—own your flaws and all.

RECEIVING LOVE IS ALLOWING SOMEONE TO GIVE YOU A GIFT

STRATEGY

Allow yourself the opportunity to share parts of your world with another person, removing some of your safeguards. Let another person love you in their way and in their time without the walls of protection. Believing you are worthy of love and becoming vulnerable will help to reveal your true self in a natural progression. Don't rush it. Pushing love to go faster is a form of self-sabotage or a path to false love that doesn't last.

Discontinue isolating yourself. Protecting your heart from being hurt also limits the possibility of truly being loved by someone else. If you're pushing others away, you are missing out on something wonderful. Receiving the gift of love will change you in such a magnificent way and is an essential ingredient to happiness.

DON'T STAY ANGRY;
DECIDE IT'S NOT FOR YOU

STRATEGY

The conflicting side of love is anger. When you get upset, it's actually healthy and can create clarity and boundaries to what you're unwilling to accept. The crucial decision is not to hold on to this feeling. Decide how you will deal with the situation and try to push forward.

Holding grudges deteriorates and erodes your ability to be happy over time. Release the feeling of anger as it begins to fade and decide continually not to hold on to the negative feeling. Acknowledge why you are feeling this way and continue to work past it.

Choosing to discontinue the feeling of being angry is a conscious decision. Once you have hold of your emotions, don't prolong those negative feelings. A good approach is to distract yourself for a while and come back to the situation when you are less emotionally charged. The moment will eventually pass; let it.

BEING KIND ISN'T A WEAKNESS; IT'S A POWERFUL STRENGTH

STRATEGY

Being kind isn't as easy as it sounds. Practice self-control and challenge yourself by removing negative attitudes and flipping them into positive ones. Look for ways to promote positive interactions and conversations.

Filter your thoughts before releasing them, especially verbal comments. Ask yourself, *Is it necessary? Is there a true benefit? Will it help the other person?* Or are you just releasing your own frustration? Withholding unkind thoughts and actions is a step in the right direction. Unkind exchanges can have a negative impact on others.

Look for opportunities to be kinder, gentler, and more compassionate to others, including strangers. Your positive inner dialogue creates internal strength by building on those powerful experiences. It's hard at first but it gets easier with practice. Remember that one kind gesture each day equals 365 kind acts a year. Small impacts add up to huge results. Be that person!

TALK MORE ABOUT THE THINGS YOU LOVE

STRATEGY

Start talking more about what you love about your day, the people in it, and the positive events that took place. Talk less about the things you disliked. Fill your space with more positive self-talk and conversations.

Begin to shift your focus and make the decision to talk about what you love and why. That's the message imprint you want to leave in your mind and the type of messages you want to leave with others when you interact, not the negative ones. People remember the last thing you said. They don't always get the updates.

You are not going to like everything and that's ok. You can begin a new trend in conversations by shifting the focus on what you love. You'll start noticing the good things and bypass the other stuff. It's contagious; you'll find that others will follow your lead. Try it—it's refreshing!

INTENTIONALLY LOOK FOR HUMOR

STRATEGY

Life can be funny; see the humor in situations. You shouldn't have to look very hard. Humor can be found at work, events, within families, and especially with friends.

Reality is funnier than any sitcom, book, or movie. Pay closer attention and look for those subtle humorous moments and insert those observations into your daily routine. Lighten your perspective on life.

People enjoy being around upbeat individuals. Talk about the lighthearted occurrences. One way to feel good about life is seeing just how funny life can be when you look through a new lens.

LAUGH AND OFTEN!

STRATEGY

Once you embrace the humor in life, laugh. Laugh until your gut hurts, your cheeks are sore from smiling, or tears are running down your face because you can't stop laughing.

Most importantly, laugh at yourself and *with* others but not *at* them. Don't take life too seriously. Find situations to giggle, smirk, smile, or laugh at all life has to offer.

If nothing else, find ways to make someone else laugh. Even think to yourself, *Now that was funny.* Laughing creates the feeling of being in a happy state of mind. Embrace it regularly.

FAMILY IS IMPORTANT, BUT YOU DECIDE HOW IMPORTANT

STRATEGY

We all know family is important, even though we don't get to pick them all. Don't take the family that you love for granted and expect that they'll always be there when you're not. Show family love, compassion, and kindness when they need it most. There are no do-overs in life.

Family isn't always biological. Remember that as an adult, you get to decide which family members are important in your life. Sometimes your friends will become your family and your family becomes your friends. Make sure you show them their value.

Just because they're family, it doesn't give them the right to mistreat you. Family members can be toxic, too, and it's ok to just walk away or take a needed break. You decide who your family is and how important that relationship is to you. You set the tone and pace. If they're good for you, see them often.

FRIENDSHIPS ARE WORTH THE INVESTMENT

STRATEGY

True friends are hard to come by; if you have three close friends, you're doing great. Friendships keep you in balance because, unlike family, they choose to be in your life. It should be a give-and-take, mutually kindred connection with common ground. Friendships are built on trust and can bring closeness to your heart.

Friends are worth having. It's wonderful to have someone by your side and know you're not alone. Friendship is about being flexible, sharing the same interests, enjoying meaningful conversations, and just doing things together.

Sometimes friends drift apart due to distance or circumstances. Usually, the most meaningful ones will withstand the test of time because the quality and trust remain intact. Friendships can be like the weather so ride out the storms and the sun will rise again. Overcoming the challenges means you both grow stronger and the bond builds deeper.

If you have any doubt if someone is truly your friend, you may already know the answer. You'll know in your gut and heart. The right friends are worth investing in so choose wisely and foster those friendships.

GIVE MORE BUT EXPECT NOTHING

STRATEGY

Give from your heart because you *want* to, not because you feel obligated to or you want credit for it. If you expect something in return, are you truly giving? Do or give something without conditions or any expectations. Be the person who gives because you care and feel good about yourself and let that be enough.

Find opportunities to give out of kindness for no reason. Try to remove the anticipation of a response, which can be difficult. Give with the thought of just giving and accept that you will not get anything in return.

Give generously while knowing and understanding that this act is completely your choice. It can give you a sense of freedom. If you expect a specific reaction, you may be left feeling disappointed.

Try volunteering, donating, or contributing in some way to something or someone else. Be part of something bigger than yourself. This is a fast and easy way to feel good about yourself and life.

STRATEGY REINFORCEMENT CHALLENGE #1

Small Reflections That Pay Compound Interest

DAY 1: FOCUS

Focus on the first three people who come to your mind. Put extra effort into each one and do something for each person to make them feel special. Make their day brighter with a small gesture, special text, email, or call to show them you are thinking of them. Reconnect or enhance the connection in a unique way.

DAY 2: REMEMBER

Remember to laugh each day. Challenge yourself to find the humor in something daily. When you start your day, look for three things that you find humorous (even if only in a thought) or at least something that made you smile. Write it down and date it with who, what, and where.

DAY 3: PRACTICE

Think of one person you admire. Write a list of all the qualities that you like about that person. Determine which qualities you have that are the same. Then identify the qualities you would like to adopt. Begin practicing at least one of them. Journal and date this challenge.

INSTRUCTIONS:

Select one challenge per day to observe the full impact. Best practice is to journal the results by the end of each day to fully process the experiences. You can pick just one or two or try all three days. The goal is to challenge yourself to do something different in order to grow.

WHEN THE NEEDS OF ONE OUTWEIGH THE NEEDS OF MANY

D o you treat yourself as well as you treat others? You may be such a dedicated caregiver that you're not sure. An essential ingredient for a happy and well-balanced lifestyle is placing your needs first, which can certainly be a challenge when taking care of the needs of others (especially children). Taking care of your needs first should override the needs of others. It's not only possible—it's critical!

It's easy making excuses when you get caught up in being there for everyone else. You fill up your life to the max with a to-do list and believe that you are too busy for yourself. At this point, the cycle continues each day until you're pushed to your full capacity.

Since being the best version of you is where it all starts, I am dedicating these strategies to self-care. They have been by far the most challenging for me, but they are essential to achieving true happiness.

The biggest payoff is taking care of yourself first, which gives you the best of both worlds. When you're at your best, you can take care of others better than you did before and still be in balance.

MIRRORS SHOW ONLY ONE PERSPECTIVE

STRATEGY

You can't always see the many magnificent things about yourself that others see. You have blind spots about yourself because you have a different view. Your view is internal while others have an external view. Your reflection in the mirror may be different than your internal emotional state. If you're feeling good about life, let it show.

Unite all the different views of your image, not just a one-sided view. Be willing to accept others' positive perspectives. Be mindful of validating and trusting the source but don't reject compliments too easily. Embrace positive feedback and recognize reputable input.

When you don't feel your best, begin by processing it with an acknowledgment. Then defuse it by flipping it, accepting all sides of yourself, and liking the true image—you. Your perspective is the only one that truly matters. When you feel good, you look good no matter what you are wearing. It's time to shine!

YOU ALWAYS MATTER!

STRATEGY

Don't subscribe to the false belief that your feelings or presence are insignificant or not important. You may just be in the wrong company. Surround yourself with acceptance. Teach others how to treat you with kindness. Don't accept anything less. It's not ok to be mistreated. Value yourself. You always matter!

PLACE YOUR HEALTH AS TOP PRIORITY

STRATEGY

Place an intense effort on meeting your needs as top priority. Remember that needs are different than wants. Needs should include eating right, physical health, mental health, and having a place to live. Wants are anything on top of these essential needs that will make your life happier each day.

Set your focus on making your physical and emotional needs a priority. This short-term investment has long-term benefits. It will make for a happier and longer life. Anything you want to change? Start today!

NO SACRIFICING!

STRATEGY

Don't place your well-being on hold for anything or anyone else. Eat meals to get your nourishment, even if it is inconvenient. Find a restroom when nature calls. Don't wait because it's not the best time. Get a good night's sleep and rest when you are exhausted. We all require these functions to live.

Taking care of yourself shouldn't be a sacrifice. Instead, it demonstrates respect for yourself. Care enough about you. You're worth it!

IT'S TIME TO RELAX

STRATEGY

Do you schedule time to relax or do you have no room in your calendar? Every day can get busy and hectic trying to juggle schedules and play beat-the-clock with life. By the time you squeeze everything into a day, you leave little or no time to relax.

Even when life gets crazy, carve out time to rejuvenate. Adopt a practice that allows you to be vigilant in setting a specific time to relax. Make this a requirement in your life. You are the only one in charge of your schedule so set aside a minimum of one hour a day.

Find things to look forward to, such as scheduling that vacation or weekend away. Plan that day off to reset your mind. Recharge so you can be in charge of your life.

BREATHE–DON'T FORGET TO BREATHE

STRATEGY

If you don't remember anything else when you get stressed, remember to take a minute to breathe. When life gets to be too much, as it does sometimes, just find a quiet place and take a breath. Take a good long, deep, deep breath and close your eyes for one minute. Focus on taking in the distraction and attempt to listen to the quiet.

This should help quiet your mind, allowing you the ability to regroup. Also, you can share this strategy with anyone else you see in crisis. You'll need the time and ability to think clearly. Breathing gives you both those things.

SLEEP—IT'S A MUST-HAVE

STRATEGY

Getting sleep is so imperative that it's worth mentioning again. With all the excitement life has to offer, sometimes you may not make sleep a high priority. Set a consistent bedtime and honor it. Create a good habit of obtaining a restful night's sleep. You'll feel the direct benefits in the morning. You'll likely wake up feeling good when you have slept well.

If you can't sleep, at least find a way to relax your mind. With some research, you can learn the many advantages to your physical and mental health when you have good sleep patterns and get rest. Even by just lying down and resting when you're unable to sleep, you still allow yourself the ability to partially reset and recharge. Clear your mind. Restore yourself. Sleep is a must!

STOP REELING AND START DISTRACTING

STRATEGY

You're *reeling* when your thoughts are stuck in a loop. When you catch yourself reeling, it's time to stop. You have come to the realization that you're wasting a great deal of time and energy on something you can't do much about. You then have two choices—either do something about it or accept it the way it is for now.

You can work on moving forward by remembering that whatever loop keeps playing over and over in your mind is temporary. Shift your focus onto something else. Give the situation a day to rest by distracting yourself with something that is more valuable and worth your time.

Chances are, the circumstances will change and you'll see the situation differently when your emotions are not running so high. Give yourself permission to let it go for now and do something else. Change your current environment, go somewhere. Make a list of things you'd rather be doing, then do one of them!

MIND SPACE IS AT CAPACITY

STRATEGY

When you feel like you have too much information or too many thoughts at once, your brain starts feeling full. Information overload can weigh you down and cause you to feel overwhelmed. At some point, you'll stop taking in information and anything after that point just won't compute in your mind. It happens but it is temporary.

Find your best method to release some information. A good option is writing it down; you can use sticky notes or journaling as an emotional release. You can also share your thoughts with a trusted source. It can be a person, computer, or your phone—whatever works for you. You'll feel so much lighter after freeing up some mind space.

Holding it all in can cause stress. Clear your mind by getting out of your head. You can use any method; just make it convenient enough for you to come back to it later. If the thought's worth revisiting, you will want to capture it. By doing this, you'll not only free up space for new thoughts but you'll also allow yourself the ability to relax a bit. You should feel a little lighter instantly.

HAVING FUN IS NOW A REQUIREMENT

STRATEGY

Make sure you carve out time to enjoy life. Are you giving yourself a break from the chaos? Be kind to yourself and do something fun. If you don't give yourself permission to, who will?

The good news is that life will still be there when you get back. It doesn't wait for you so take some free time for yourself. Go get that special cup of coffee or tea, go for a walk, make time for your hobby, hang out with friends, or go somewhere and do something you've been waiting to. Just remember to have fun!

Make sure you have a good work-life balance. Instill in your mind that life is to be enjoyed. Go out there and make sure you are living it.

DO THE IMPOSSIBLE–UNPLUG, BE UNAVAILABLE

STRATEGY

This strategy is easy to say but harder to do. You don't always need to accommodate others. Allow yourself to disconnect periodically from all electronic devices, particularly text messages, emails, and calls. You simply can't be available all the time so from time to time be unavailable.

Avoid being too available and accessible 100 percent of the time; it is a fast energy drain. Find a way to unplug on a specific day and time for several hours or for the entire day. Make it a weekly or monthly habit. Put it on your calendar to ensure it happens. Juice up your own battery and you'll feel a sense of freedom and recharge.

Once you get used to it, others will begin to accept that there are times when you can't be reached. They will learn when it's time to get ahold of you and in your space. You set the tone. Enjoy some uninterrupted time to yourself and adopt the "unplug" philosophy. It will help destress your life when you occasionally unplug.

KEEP THE FRONT DOOR OPEN

STRATEGY

When you're not open to new thoughts or ideas, you are closed off. Open your front door to different thoughts or possibilities. Make room for new ways of thinking, new ideas, and new interactions. When you are not open, you likely isolate yourself by thinking you are protecting yourself. This means that others must enter your world through the side door or even the back door and only the select few can enter your life. This can make your world small and possibly lonely.

Use good judgment but be mindful not to lock the front door. If your front door is locked, no new possibilities can enter your life. Open the front door once in a while to allow some unknown happiness inside. By selectively allowing new visitors inside your life, you give the opportunity for new ideas and experiences to feel alive. Openness is an essential ingredient to happiness.

STRATEGY REINFORCEMENT CHALLENGE #2

When the Needs of One Outweigh the Needs of Many

DAY 1: FOCUS

Focus on giving yourself permission to enjoy life. Unplug, go outside, go for a drive, go to a beach or lake, do whatever it takes to relax. Focus on having some *me* time. Challenge yourself to do this once a week by giving yourself permission to have fun. Create this habit to rejuvenate.

DAY 2: REMEMBER

When stressed, practice shifting gears. Redirect your thoughts and replace them with new nouns (people, places, or things) that give you positive input. Read, go for a walk, watch TV, or hang out with someone. Remember that your thoughts are a direct link to your perception and attitude. Redirect yourself.

DAY 3: PRACTICE

If you could change one thing about yourself, what would it be? Why would you change it? What stops you from making this change? Create the rationales to make it happen or ask for help. Look for small ways to take action to be your best self. You're the only one who can. Practice until it becomes part of you.

INSTRUCTIONS:

Select one challenge per day to observe the full impact. Best practice is to journal the results by the end of each day to fully process the experiences. Pick just one or two or try all three days. The goal is to challenge yourself to do something different in order to grow.

EACH CONNECTION LENDS TO A VAST NETWORK

Once you discover the benefits of taking care of yourself, having healthy and fulfilling relationships becomes clearer and easier. Each person in your life is a connection that frames your support system in some way and builds your network.

Life experiences are enriched by sharing your life space. You get to assign seats and give consent to how many will be sitting at your table. You must define the value that each person brings because you have limited seating. Don't fill in all the seats at once; reserve a few for those surprise guests. You never know who is going to show up unannounced and be an influential game-changer. You determine the right amount, and you can limit seating when it starts to deplete the quality of the interactions you are having.

You have only so much time and attention that can be divided. Place the people most important to you in high priority seats. Be selective and include the right people, with the right amount of time, and at the right time. Whether an intimate relationship, family member, friend, or professional relationship, these next strategies can be assigned to anyone. True happiness is doing what you love surrounded by the people you love. This makes all your connections complete!

LIFE IS TO BE SHARED

STRATEGY

You'll have moments when you need to be alone but many times you can share your experiences with others. Find your balance between self-reflection and time to include others. Too much of either can cause you to be out of balance.

Don't be afraid of including someone else or making a new friend to create memorable moments during those unforgettable experiences. You can experience many special moments that include someone else. Make plans with someone and give yourself something to look forward to.

Experience life with others; life is to be shared. It makes life more meaningful. Don't wait for them to ask you; go out and find some entertainment with someone else!

FORGIVENESS: FREE YOURSELF

STRATEGY

Forgiveness isn't a one-time thing; it's something you keep working on until the issue is resolved in the best possible way for you to move on. Work on letting it go. Forgiving doesn't mean that situation or person is back in your life. You don't forget what happened, but you learn the life lesson that it was meant to teach you.

How does holding a grudge ever help? It doesn't resolve the issue but it does prolong the pain. You end up missing gaps of time you'll never get back when you hold a grudge. There is no wrong or right way to forgive; just make peace with it so it doesn't slowly eat you up inside.

The gift of forgiveness is really for you, not for anyone else. It allows the opportunity to move on without holding on. Reconcile your past decisions and figure out what you would do differently, then release them.

ASSUMPTIONS CREATE BARRIERS

STRATEGY

Your brain will naturally want to fill in the gaps, and you'll likely draw inaccurate conclusions about situations and people from what you think you "know" to be true. You begin to believe you have the full story and then continue to make decisions based on what you "think" you know. However, assumptions cause limitations so fight the urge!

The truth is that you'll only get to know part of the story most of the time, unless you keep digging. The story stops with the last piece of information you were given or have access to. Most of the time you'll find out later that there is more to the story.

You probably know the saying about people who assume. If it's bothering you, find out the rest of the story. Decide that you'll make no more assumptions and instead be a fact finder.

ACTION OR NONACTION SPEAKS THE SAME VOLUME

STRATEGY

Others will do or say things to poke and prod you for a reaction. Sometimes the best reaction is to take no action. Not reacting is very powerful and can speak louder than any words chosen.

Remember that you don't always have to respond. Immediate responses can be overrated and impulsive; your first thought may not be your final one, especially when it is emotionally driven.

How many times have you said to yourself, *I wish I would have said this*? You can wait to process your thoughts and feelings to ensure they match, but the trick is not to wait too long. Use your best judgment or ask for an option. If action is needed, then don't wait. It will depend on the situation so choose wisely.

BUILDING THE RIGHT RELATIONSHIPS

STRATEGY

Look for opportunities to strengthen the connections with people you enjoy being around. Find ways to make new professional connections or personal friendships. Everyone is good at something. Look for ways to include others instead of excluding them.

You can't survive in this world alone. You'll need other people for certain things. No one is good at everything, so find ways to build on ideas or projects by including someone else. Teamwork at home or at your job can make you feel connected with others while learning new things and learning about yourself.

Keep adding to your team of supporters and be supportive. Go out there and create stronger bonds. Build those important relationships; you won't regret it.

RESPECT LIFE, YOURSELF, AND OTHERS

STRATEGY

Respect is a display of courtesy for life that you can give yourself and others. Showing others respect should be common practice unless it's lost in some way. If it isn't tarnished, give it freely. You'll get it back, even if it's not from the person you expect. It says a lot about you when you honor others as human beings. It also says a lot about other people when they are not respectful in return.

Most importantly, respect yourself! Be who you are with dignity and grace. You don't have to prove yourself to anyone. Respect is a form of love and kindness. Be that person who respects all walks of life.

ACCEPT RESPONSIBILITY

STRATEGY

Accept your own part or role in a situation whenever the outcome is less than desirable. If you contributed in any way, figure out what part you played. Backtrack how your actions or lack of actions affected the situation. Remember that you have the power to propel things into a different direction by acknowledging and accepting responsibility. Own it and make things right.

LIMITED RELATIONSHIPS

STRATEGY

You will have different attributes to offer in different relationships. You can't expect everyone to have the same expectations you do. Without defining the roles, accept that some relationships will have limits. Unless you plan on a relationship being significant to you in some way, limited relationships are where they all start. Just know that your expectation and theirs may not match all the time and accept it.

If you are seeking an unlimited relationship, make sure the other person is on the same page. Talk to them about your expectations and know theirs too. The bottom line is that it's ok to have limited relationships. Having this mindset helps avoid being disappointed. If the relationship becomes too limited, reevaluate, have a conversation, or let it go and move on.

DON'T TAKE IT PERSONALLY

STRATEGY

You never know what someone else is going through so don't jump to conclusions that it's you. You don't know everything about the other person's life to understand what could be causing an unknown interference in your interaction with them. You may not get to know everything about their story, and the struggle during interactions may not be about you. Unless you are having your own struggles, don't absorb it. Let it roll off your back. Regardless, their actions say more about them than they do about you. Move on and move forward!

SET YOUR PREFERENCES

STRATEGY

Be selective about whom you have in your life. Always choose quality over quantity when surrounding yourself with people. Don't just fall into relationships; set your preferences. Honor your preferences by spending your time with quality individuals. You get to decide when and where to spend your time and for how long. If you have good people surrounding you, your state of happiness will certainly improve. Be selective! You decide.

REMAIN HUMBLE

STRATEGY

Even when things are going well in life, remain appreciative and gracious. Support others who work hard and who are in it for the right reasons. You may be transparent even when you think you're not. Being humble with integrity and dignity is a beautiful thing. Others will appreciate the lack of arrogance. Embrace the positive spirit of being grateful. Stay grounded even in your wins.

STRATEGY REINFORCEMENT CHALLENGE #3

Each Connection Lends to a Vast Network

DAY 1: FOCUS

Focus on not complaining in your daily conversations. Focus on *what's right* or the good in situations and bypass the *what's wrong* topics. You'll notice others will follow your lead and conversations will be more positive, naturally. Be the one who sees what's right instead of what's wrong.

DAY 2: REMEMBER

As you interact with others in your life, remember to start taking inventory. Are the people closest to you the people with whom you want to surround yourself? If someone is high maintenance all the time, consider *fading* (allowing time to pass between interactions) to see if they should remain in your close circle.

DAY 3: PRACTICE

Think of that one person who irritates you the most. Now think of three positive attributes or skills this person has. Yes, you can. Dig deep. All people have talents, but generally it's a personality clash that may causes you to dislike someone. Although you can't change that person, you can change your perspective of them by observing another side of them.

INSTRUCTIONS:

Select one challenge per day to observe the full impact. Best practice is to journal the results by the end of each day to fully process the experiences. Pick just one or two or try all three days. The goal is to challenge yourself to do something different in order to grow.

A WHISPER IN THE MOMENT CAN ECHO THROUGH A LIFETIME

Communication is pivotal to having any type of successful relationship. It is the driving force of how you interact in your daily life. You strive to convey your message in hopes that you are sending it accurately. The content and the method of your communication, therefore, need to be considered heavily.

Being aware of how you deliver your messages sets you up for having productive communications. Consider massaging your thoughts before they turn into messages. Listen to the word formation of your internal unspoken voice.

Your tone doesn't need to be loud or overpowering to be heard; it needs to contain the right information at the right time. Your declaration needs to be meaningful to be powerful. A mindful whisper or a well-thought-out communication can overpower a boisterous blast of BS. These are the messages that echo back to you in a subtle whisper throughout your life and the ones you're likely to pass on.

Being intentional with your word choices when communicating is such a monumental craft that I devote these next pages in honor of its importance. If you care about the outcome of your messages, be conscious of their meaning and let your whispers echo.

LISTEN—THAT'S ALL YOU HAVE TO DO

STRATEGY

The most crucial element to communication by far is truly listening without formulating a response or critiquing the content of someone else's information. Listening allows the ability to absorb 100 percent of the message being sent. It's vital in all conversations.

If you are listening at anything less than 100-percent capacity, you are receiving only a partial message. This leaves room for plenty of misunderstandings. Be a good listener—it's that simple.

TURN ON YOUR FILTER-BEFORE YOU SAY IT!

STRATEGY

Thoughts may pop in your head often, but you *must* use a filter before sharing them. As you're sharing your thoughts, you are live and life has no delete button. Before you give in to your impulse to blurt them out, ask yourself:

1.   Are they helpful?

2.   Do they prevent something bad from happening?

3.   Will they have a positive impact?

Consider your thoughts first and the impact they may have. If you feel in your heart or gut that they need to be said, then do so with the right intentions. Saying something in anger could distort your message, and it generally causes only pain and regret.

Just because you think it, that doesn't mean you should share it. Be watchful of your words and choose to share them wisely. Words do have an impact, even when you are not aware of it.

Keep your filter on at all times!

HARD TRUTHS ARE BETTER THAN EASY LIES

STRATEGY

Telling someone what they want to hear is easy in the moment but ultimately could have a negative long-term consequence or impact. Staying as close to the truth as possible is the best option so that the other person can make an informed decision and neither one of you will have to backtrack.

As you aim to move forward in life, steer toward the truth when deciding if that little white lie is best. It's all on what you share, how much you share, and how you deliver the message that matters.

BE CAREFUL WHEN ASKING THAT QUESTION

STRATEGY

Be prepared when asking a question because you may not get the answer you're looking for. If you are truly not prepared to receive the answer, you could be disappointed. Asking a question just for the sake of asking isn't really showing interest if you are truly not interested in the answer. Instead, it shows the other person that you are disingenuous.

Brace yourself for another person's truth or a different perspective, not just the answer you wanted to hear. Others around you will have different views and you will always find more that you haven't considered. If it's an important question you're asking, be careful whom you are asking and value their input. Only ask the question if you truly want the answer.

SAY "I'M SORRY"–DON'T BE AFRAID TO APOLOGIZE

STRATEGY

It's better to say "I'm sorry" when you know it is for the other person as well as for yourself. Remove your pride and apologize. It could end up being the one thing you wish you had said when it ends up being too late. Just remember to say it with feeling; if you don't feel it, neither will the other person.

Apologizing doesn't mean that you're weak but it does mean that you care. It takes only a second but can have a meaningful impact when speaking from the heart. If the other person is important to you, saying the important words "I'm sorry" is worth it.

"THANK YOU"–SAY IT LIKE YOU MEAN IT

STRATEGY

You may sometimes forget to say or show appreciation for the little or big things people do for you, but don't take anything for granted. Express your appreciation, no matter how small the gesture, by saying "thank you." If it means that someone was thinking of you, express your gratitude with feeling. It may mean a whole lot to the other person. Acknowledge their effort and say it like a champion.

WORD CHOICE MATTERS

STRATEGY

You will find times when you need to be extremely aware of your word choices. Become more aware of how and when you use words, including the tone of your delivery and the message. The selection of your words is important so that they match your actual meaning. They matter more to the audience and to the timing of delivery. Also, be aware of your environment and who else is around.

You may be unaware of how words affect others, and they can leave a negative impact when you are not careful. This could happen even without your knowing or realizing it. You can watch facial expressions after the delivery but they're not always a giveaway. Words are very powerful, so say what you mean and mean what you say!

FIND YOUR FAVORITE WORD

STRATEGY

A goal to help keep you focused and inspired is to identify your favorite word. This word should make you feel good inside whenever you say it, hear it, or see it. It can be a focal point when you need a distraction, when you're stressed, or when you need a little motivation.

What is your favorite word?

When you need to refocus to get your mind unstuck, visualize your word. Better yet, be creative. Make it visible by printing it out, and then incorporate seeing it as part of your daily routine. Find a picture or mental image that represents this word. Put it on your desktop, cellphone, or any place that only you can see it each morning. Make sure you *feel* this word and that what it represents to you is meaningful.

AVOID WORD BOMBS

STRATEGY

You will find that people sometimes throw word bombs by flinging out words or statements that trigger or rub you the wrong way. They will say things you didn't see coming. During these times, the word bombs can cause emotional surges so you will need to rise to the occasion. They can undoubtedly present challenging circumstances.

You *always* have a choice to not respond. If you see no direct benefit of your contribution to the conversation or your reaction, then choose to be silent and walk away. Ride the wave. Sit this one out. Make them wonder what you're thinking; it can be very powerful to be mysterious.

Another option is to preplan your response if you anticipate one of these bombs being flung at you. You can craft a well-thought-out response that defuses the bomb immediately, usually involving the use of humor. The best defense is rising above it.

Life has a funny way of changing the circumstances, which is one thing you can count on. The people who target you see something they like but can't have. You can avoid the landmines; step around them.

KNOWING WHAT NOT TO SAY

STRATEGY

Knowing what *not* to say is just as important as knowing what to say. If you can't find the right words at the right time, it's fine to let the moment pass. You can't ever take words back. Sometimes just being there for someone is enough; it can speak volumes.

If you don't know what to say, consider a thoughtful delayed approach. Keeping things simple is enough. You may find a card or a song that says it better. Agonizing to find the right words can be frustrating, and it's fine just being in the moment and not saying anything. Sometimes the presence of a person says it all.

ACCEPTING SILENCE

STRATEGY

Practice accepting the absence of sound, specifically when no one is talking. When you are given the gift of silence, enjoy the moment. Attempt to redirect your thoughts into positive self-talk or productive planning in your mind. It's ok not to talk or not to engage in a conversation. Even if someone asks you a question, that doesn't mean you have to answer it.

If something makes you feel uncomfortable, you're not required to respond. The moment will pass so let it. Accepting silence is giving your mind space to think and process other things. It really works! Silence also leaves the other person wondering what you are thinking, and in most cases, that is a good thing.

IT'S OK TO SAY NO

STRATEGY

Give yourself permission to say, "not today," "maybe some other time," "thanks for thinking of me," "can I take a raincheck?," or simply, "no." It's also ok to have a date with yourself or simply honor your decision not to do anything. If you'd rather not, it's ok to say, "no, thank you." It's no one else's business what you do with your time. It's your time and you get to decide how you want to spend it.

If it's work related, stand up for what you think is right or what makes the best business sense. Saying no can make people take notice, but it can also create a healthy conversation. It's all in how you say no that matters. It's not always easy, but it's worth it, so go ahead and say no.

THE TRUTH

STRATEGY

You owe it to yourself to be honest with others and yourself. Once you know your truth, own it. The untold truth will always surface—maybe not today or tomorrow but it will. If you deal with the truth now, no one can take away that power or hold you hostage emotionally. The truth is easy to remember. Tell it with a little grace and compassion.

This doesn't mean you have to divulge all the details but you can decide what matters most to the situation. Don't use the truth as a weapon to hurt someone; doing that will guarantee a bad ending. Face the truth and move forward and then you don't have to look back. Stay as close to the truth as possible because it's worth telling.

STRATEGY REINFORCEMENT CHALLENGE #4

A Whisper in the Moment Can Echo through a Lifetime

DAY 1: FOCUS

Focus on the content of your message. Ask yourself what your message is and what impression you want your audience to be left with at the end of the conversation or communication. Focus on massaging your thoughts before delivery to become a mindful messenger. Be intentional with your words.

DAY 2: REMEMBER

Remember that it's fine to decline. Saying no can be challenging but it's all in the approach. Be confident and kind when saying it. "I'll catch you next time" or "I would love to but I have plans" are good examples of declining gracefully. Predesign your "no, thanks" statements and kept them in your back pocket.

DAY 3: PRACTICE

Practice challenging yourself with previous missed messages. Reflect on miscommunications, misunderstandings, or messages that got misinterpreted. See this as an opportunity to recraft a new delivery. What would you do next time to convey a better and more mindful message? Practice and often!

INSTRUCTIONS:

Select one challenge per day to observe the full impact. Best practice is to journal the results by the end of each day to fully process the experiences. Pick just one or two or try all three days. The goal is to challenge yourself to do something different in order to grow.

SEEDS OF AMBITION ARE THE FRUIT OF SUCCESS

It's time to focus on your ambitions and compile your list of goals. Goals give you direction, just like a road map that leads you to a precise location. They guide you to fulfill your purpose of finding happiness while achieving your success stories.

The best way to achieve a goal is to assign actions to it. The tasks are the seeds, and as you complete each one, you begin watering the seeds of success.

Most goals are not attainable instantaneously, so having a solid approach keeps you moving in the right direction and can alleviate you from feeling overwhelmed or stressed out. The actions turn into the fruits of your labor. Watch as your ambition grows and takes you closer to hitting your target.

The next set of benefits is dedicated to the goal-setting tips I've found to be most useful and beneficial in my life.

HOCUS-FOCUS!

STRATEGY

Wherever you place your thoughts and attention will become your focus. Keep your goals in sight. Knowing what you want and getting there can be the hardest part. Achievement takes determination and dedication with an unwavering focus. Keep reviewing your plan; be flexible but stay on target.

Life is full of distractions. Carve out time to filter your thoughts and clear your mind. Knowing what you don't want is part of the process. Don't subscribe to the naysayers who don't see your vision. Instead, let them fuel you. Remember that you will have obstacles. Jump over them or find a way around them. Just don't give up! This is your dream, so focus on making it happen. You're the only one who can.

PATIENCE: BE THE PERSON WHO HAS SOME

STRATEGY

Be patient with others as well as yourself. Practice enhancing your level of patience by giving yourself some larger doses of tolerance. Don't expect more from yourself than you would from someone else. Also, don't expect more from someone else than you would be willing to give.

Anything worth having doesn't come easily or everyone would have it. Having patience may seem like a dying trait, but you can be the one who rejuvenates it in a situation. It takes inner strength to be patient, and it's well worth the investment. Be that person.

THE PAST CAN BE LIKE QUICKSAND; DON'T GET STUCK

STRATEGY

You will have moments in your life that you can't forget, specific unfond memories from the past. Remembering the hurt and pain from those experiences is a part of growing and evolving, but staying stuck in them leaves no room for any new experiences to replace them. Learn to accept the past. You can't change it, but you can let it go.

Memories fade, so allow the bad ones to leave and then embark on the journey to heal from them. Stop holding on so tight to the past that is there is no room for the future. It's time to create new memories. Don't let the past define you. Be enlightened by it but don't stay there. Make room for the present!

GIVING UP IS EASY, SO DON'T!

STRATEGY

Don't give up when a situation, a task, or life gets too hard. Just take a break and rethink a new strategy. People give up every day, but those who keep going achieve their goals. It's easy to quit and walk away.

Jump over those hurdles that life throws at you. It's harder to overcome challenges, but if it's worth doing, don't give up! Press on and make it happen. Be the one that people admire because you inspire.

PAY ATTENTION TO THE DETAILS

STRATEGY

Life is full of many details that provide us clues along the way. Take the time to absorb the fine points of life and the people around you. Notice the uniqueness of the people, places, and things that makes them distinct and significant.

The many details will accumulate to something magnificent, so pay close attention to see if they either align with or repel your goals. Examine closely the path you're on to achieve your goals and you will see signs along the way. The trail you're blazing will have details in the form of signs that can lead you right to your goals and dreams. Even if the signs have you turning around or they lead you in a new direction, pay attention. You'll get there!

FLEXIBILITY MUSCLE

STRATEGY

Being flexible is the opposite of being stubborn. Flex the muscle of your perspectives to see things differently and make things work. It's ok to have a plan but be bendable when things don't go exactly your way.

If you want to overcome life hurdles quickly, embrace the ability to be agile. It's ok to bend sometimes, if you know when and how far. Incorporating this trait can reduce stress. Find your balance in how flexible you need to be to obtain your goals without compromising your dignity or principles.

BE SPONTANEOUS SOMETIMES

STRATEGY

Typically, the most memorable moments in life are the ones that are unplanned. Planning is something I thrive on so this one is a big challenge for me to overcome. The best experiences in my life have been the small miracles that have happened when I've incorporated being spontaneous and deciding to live in the moment.

Get outside of your head and enjoy the feeling of being free in the moment when being spontaneous. The possibilities that exist become endless! Embrace the unexpected.

MONEY, MONEY, AND MORE MONEY

STRATEGY

Money is tricky because you need it now and you'll need it later. You should spend money on necessities first but also save some money for later, in case those unexpected situations pop up. You can budget and plan for both. Purchase items you need to live and can afford.

Learn the money-balance dance. Make more money than you spend. Spend less than you earn. Pay your bills first. Know the difference between *want* and *need* when spending your hard-earned cash. Fad items will fade, so don't be fooled. A place to live, food, and daily necessities are required; the rest are just things we buy. Whenever possible, save some money—you'll always need it.

FACE FEARS WITH A PLAN

STRATEGY

You may have certain things in life that you avoid, that make you feel uncomfortable, or that you downright fear. Some fears will likely have a greater effect on you than others. If you have a fear that you need to face, follow this plan.

Find a support person who has faced this fear already or someone who supports you in life. Identify one method that will help to improve the experience, then work on finding another, and so on. Fear is ruled by an unknown outcome and the feeling of not being in control. To help overcome a fear, settle on a plan and include a support person. If you can face the worse possible scenario, then you've got it! Don't be ruled by fear and don't face it alone.

SLOW DOWN, SLOW YOUR ROLL

STRATEGY

Is it better to have things done or to have them done right? Checking items off a to-do list feels great but rushing through the items leaves room for errors or missed steps. Don't bypass an opportunity to have something done with no regrets; it doesn't usually come back down the road.

Enjoy the journey of accomplishment instead of rushing through life. Slow things down a notch when you notice the finished product isn't your best. Be your best and do your best!

FOCUS ON WHAT YOU CAN DO

STRATEGY

It is natural and easy to find things that you can't do, don't like, or can't prevent. Instead, challenge your thinking to focus on the one thing you *can* do or change. Once you create this habit of shifting your focus, you will be surprised by the impact it has. Regularly practice filling in the blanks below in your thoughts:

I can't do _____ [this], but I can do _____ [this].

Practice regulating your thoughts with producing actions that will make a positive difference until it becomes second nature. It can become automatic to say that you can't do something, which can then translate to you won't or you're unwilling to do something. It's much more powerful to focus on the things you're willing to do and to keep your attention on what you can do!

BOUNDARIES: KNOW YOURS AND THEIRS

STRATEGY

Think of boundaries the same way you consider walls in your home. They are needed to separate space. Don't find exceptions to remove the separators (walls) that are your boundaries. Empower yourself and hold strong to the boundaries you set. This is how you teach people how to treat you. Define what you are willing and unwilling to accept from others and know your own limits. You'll respect yourself and feel good about yourself when you honor your own boundaries.

ALWAYS DO YOUR BEST

STRATEGY

Strive to always do your best and don't second-guess yourself. Appreciate that you won't always be on top of your game but still do your best. Even if you're not at your best, it's ok to acknowledge it. Knowing the difference is respecting yourself. Do the best you can in that very moment. Don't live with regrets! Do what you can do, the best you can. Be the best at being you.

STAYING POSITIVE ISN'T EASY!

STRATEGY

At first, becoming a positive thinker is challenging. Staying positive is even tougher. Nonetheless, once you train your brain to find the good in a bad situation, it gets easier. You will begin to form a good habit.

It's easy to be negative and much more difficult to be positive. It's natural to see all the things that are wrong. As you live in an imperfect world, look for the things that are right and shift your focus there. It's where your thoughts land that become your reality. You'll feel better about yourself if you stay positive, and you'll find that it is contagious!

STRATEGY REINFORCEMENT CHALLENGE #5

Seeds of Ambition Are the Fruit of Success

DAY 1: FOCUS

Setting goals starts with focusing on your top three goals. Having too many goals leads to uncompleted goals. Focus on what's most important, order your goals by priority, and decide your next step for each goal. Focus on what *needs* to be done versus what you *want* to do. Use this method as a filter.

DAY 2: REMEMBER

Remember that if you get stuck while attaining a goal, make a step-by-step plan by breaking down the goal into smaller tasks. Get support if it causes you to feel overwhelmed. Remember to work on one goal at a time and start with the one that will have the most impact. Get unstuck, revise your plan. Move forward!

DAY 3: PRACTICE

Practice staying in the positive zone. Think of one thing you're grateful for daily. It is impossible to feel grateful and unhappy at the same time. Shift your thoughts onto what you can do versus what you can't do. Look for the positive in a bad situation and find the positive outcome. Journal and date this challenge.

INSTRUCTIONS:

Select one challenge per day to observe the full impact. Best practice is to journal the results by the end of each day to fully process the experiences. Pick just one or two or try all three days. The goal is to challenge yourself to do something different in order to grow.

A GOOD CHOICE NOW LAYS THE FOUNDATION OF PROSPERITY

Making decisions keeps your goals in alignment while juggling the balls of life. As goals give you direction, your decisions will get you to your destination. Sometimes making the wrong decision can put you off course. You can get lost or worse, even end up in the middle of nowhere, but each decision is an opportunity to learn something and can get you back on course.

Trust your gut, and don't avoid decisions to become stagnant. Break down bigger decisions into smaller incremental ones. Every decision should move you toward your goal. Just be careful not to be too hasty and make a major decision that lands you in a mucked-up mess.

You can make decisions more easily by selecting results that endorse your goals while being your true self. The following strategies are designed to give you easy payoff benefits during the decision-making process with successful results. Go for it!

ALIGN YOUR PRIORITIES

STRATEGY

As you make decisions, ask yourself what is more important in the long run. Fill in the blanks:

Is _____ more important than _____?

For example:

Is watching a movie more important than sleep?

Will you possibly regret your decision later?

Is your decision based on your current emotional state?

Keep in mind when making decisions involving other people that you can't be everywhere or everything to everyone. What is best for you and how will it affect the other person? Only you know the answer.

THE UNKNOWN ZONE

STRATEGY

Generally, the biggest obstacle in making a decision is analyzing the *unknown zone*. You may worry, get scared, or allow "what if" statements to creep in and cause anxiety because you don't know the answer. At this crossroad, you may avoid making a decision or possibly wait until someone else makes it for you. This is probably not the best approach.

If you don't know the answer yet, then what information do you need? Reach out and find it or someone who might know. There is always someone out there who knows more than you. Research it. Don't fear the unknown zone—this zone wakes you up. Go out there and conquer it!

INSTANT GRATIFICATION: IS IT WORTH IT?

STRATEGY

Having something right now by obtaining immediate possessions in hope of instant happiness is becoming the social norm. Even though at times you feel like you can't wait, it's better to think about your decision. Consider if it really makes sense before rushing into it or if you're just giving in to that feeling of having it now.

Have you ever had buyer's remorse? Wish you hadn't been so impulsive in your actions? Learn the privilege of the process of first being able to think it through, investigate further, or simply do the math to confirm if it's right. The moments of false happiness with those quick decisions can be short-lived. It's ok to wait for the right time and have it the right way. It creates true appreciation and sincere gratification.

OVERPOWERING EMOTIONAL IMPULSES

STRATEGY

Being the first or the fastest isn't always better. Knowing what's the right thing for you or when it's the best time will win you the top spot in life. Don't be so quick to respond to emails, text messages, social media, or calls when certain messages emotionally surge you. Gain composure over your impulse to react and then reply in your best frame of mind with your best response.

Practice refraining from immediate responses; contemplate your thoughts before delivery. Test-drive this to see if you get a different result than you expected. Usually your first thought isn't your last one. It's natural to want to know something out of curiosity, but unless it's an emergency, allow yourself some space to process new information if it causes you to surge emotionally. Having the best response brings you the best outcome. Overpower the urge when surged!

TOO MUCH OF A GOOD THING ISN'T ALWAYS A GOOD THING

STRATEGY

Practice moderation in everything, use portion control, and sometimes give others some space. Everything has a limit. Being with someone or doing something *all* the time deteriorates its value. Too much of a person, situation, work, etc. can depreciate the joy it brings. You may end up taking it for granted and liking it less. Savor the moments you do have while allowing time to accumulate in between so that they sustain their worth. Too much of a good thing ends up being not a good thing, so find the balance.

WHAT'S SO IMPORTANT ABOUT BEING RIGHT?

STRATEGY

What is the real benefit of being right all the time? What price will you have to pay? Always ask yourself when you are at a crossroads or in a difficult conversation if it's the time to be right or if you should let it go to have peace. If you know you're right, can't that be enough in a situation? Unless it changes the outcome, choose to have peace.

You will have times when being right is the most important aspect to the circumstance, so stay mindful of getting through those moments and whose joy you're stepping on. Being right can feel great in the moment but know the price you may pay and remember to enjoy life. You will see the difference between knowing you're right and letting everyone else know you're right. Enjoy life with knowing you're right!

DON'T ACT IN DOUBT; TRUST YOUR GUT!

STRATEGY

If you have any doubt about a decision, that means something is holding you back. If you hesitate, evaluate. Don't make a decision when you're unsure, unless you have no other choice. If you don't have time to evaluate, then trust your instincts. Sometimes it's better not to act than to regret it later. Trust yourself enough to know when it's time to act and when not to. Life has no take-backs or undo buttons. Listen to your inner voice. Don't doubt yourself; trust yourself!

IF YOU DON'T KNOW, JUST SAY SO

STRATEGY

Remain humble and honest enough to admit when you don't know something. It's an opportunity to learn and connect with someone who does know. Bring others into your world. Investigate it further with some research. The answers are out there. Don't be too quick to say "I know" when you may not know.

With help you can climb mountains, but sometimes it's necessary to start at the bottom while someone else holds out their hand to help pull you up the rest of the way. Reach out your hand and accept the help. It's ok not to know everything; just say you don't know.

INFORMATION OVERLOAD

STRATEGY

When you're feeling that you've received too much information, don't hold on to it all. Keeping a magnitude of information in your head can produce anxiety and tension. When this happens, it's time to filter and sort it out by releasing some information.

You can free up space in your memory bank. Write some information down, text it to yourself, or use a computer or tablet to release the feeling of information overload. If you decide to share the information during a conversation, be mindful of whom you choose, especially if you're sharing someone else's information. Be careful when sharing another person's story and consider their feelings. You take in lots of information every day, so choose wisely the information you retain. Save the important stuff and let go of the rest.

YOU'RE NOT TOO BUSY

STRATEGY

The only person in charge of your schedule is you. How you decide to spend your time is up to you. If you hear yourself saying "I'm too busy" continually, then you may need to make some quick adjustments. Stop making excuses and start carving out some time. It's your decision how you fill up your days, so be selective in how you spend your time.

You will need gaps of time to regroup and a simple strategy to pull some free time into your life. Block out time to relax and unwind so that you're not too busy. Yes, you're allowed. You can't do it all so stop trying. It's all about setting your priorities.

LET IT GO!

STRATEGY

You have the power to decide if you should let some things go or if you need to address them. Is a situation or person causing you too much undue stress? Is it worth it? If not, place your time and energy into something more productive and worthwhile. What is the benefit of holding on to this circumstance if it is not causing you happiness? If the situation will not matter in the long run or even next week, let it go! Keep moving forward.

REMOVE EXPECTATIONS; BE OPEN TO POSSIBILITIES

STRATEGY

To truly enjoy an experience, remove the idea of how things are supposed to go. If you're not open-minded enough to manage the unexpected, you are setting yourself up for possible disappointment. If you aim to have peace and harmony in your life, resist the temptation to force your own expectations onto others.

Establish your wish list as a great starting point but be open to all possibilities. Don't limit yourself. Try removing predetermined expectations when life changes the plan.

STRATEGY REINFORCEMENT CHALLENGE #6

A Good Choice Now Lays the Foundations of Prosperity

DAY 1: FOCUS

Focus aligning your priorities with your three goals from strategy reinforcement challenge #5 (page 78). Rank your three goals in order of importance. If your priorities and goals don't align, revise your goals until they match. Stay focused and keep making the decision to work on your goals and the meaning behind each one.

DAY 2: REMEMBER

Remember that you're in charge of your schedule but you can't do it all. Goals are great to achieve but make sure to enjoy the journey. Carve out some me time. Select a day or a few hours to set aside on your calendar to relax. Do one fun thing a week at a minimum or rest for a couple hours. Make this a habit.

DAY 3: PRACTICE

Practice making decisions that make you feel comfortable. It's wonderful to have solid expectations but make room for some flexibility. Incorporate being adaptable while identifying what is most important. Practice filling in these blanks: Is it more important to _____ than to _____?

INSTRUCTIONS

Select one challenge per day to observe the full impact. Best practice is to journal the results by the end of each day to fully process the experiences. Pick just one or two or try all three days. The goal is to challenge yourself to do something different in order to grow.

7

ONE-DEGREE SHIFTS NAVIGATE TO AN AUTHENTIC TRUE SELF

Accept nothing less than being your authentic true self. The most important aspect of life is figuring out who you are and what you want because it continuously changes. You evolve from the day you are born until this very moment.

It's time to see yourself through a clear lens.

A key reason your vision may get clouded is that you go through so many stages in life, such as childhood, adolescence, and adulthood. You will also experience many layers in between. You'll encounter so many mini shifts in who and what impacts you. The different stages can lead to a state of confusion and you are left to sort it all out.

The secret to finding your own happiness is adjusting your sail to find the right direction, making small incremental shifts until things fit into place. Bigger corrections may cause unnecessary waves and can get your sails turned around, leaving you to make more difficult life adjustments.

Make sure you have the right coordinates with any minor adjustments to keep you on course. Ultimately, you are the captain in charge of sailing your own ship.

SELF-ACCEPTANCE WITH NO CONDITIONS

STRATEGY

Accepting who you are and what you are is having unconditional love and kindness for yourself. It's a gift you owe to you. Learn to accept all aspects of who you are without exceptions, not just all your amazing attributes. Accept all the flaws and imperfections that make you, you.

It's easy to be blinded by your own perception of yourself. Give yourself some credit, even though it may feel foreign at first. If you often criticize yourself for not having something, or for what you did or didn't do right, or for not being at a certain point in your life by a certain age, remember that it's all in your head. There is no wrong way to be you!

Accept yourself for who you are right now. You are already working on yourself by reading this book. Love who you are today, not who you will be tomorrow. This is the most important part of the journey.

YOUR REVIEW OF YOUR STARRING ROLE

STRATEGY

When you are struggling in a specific situation, look at your own contributions to it. Thoughtfully revisit the role you played. If you can dig deep and reach inside yourself, then you may find the solution. With an honest but positive spirit, start by asking yourself these three questions:

1. In what way did I contribute to this situation?

2. What would I change about my role or the decisions I made?

3. Am I shifting the blame onto someone else or defending my role?

Be the hero; acknowledge your part and own it. Offer up an alternative solution. When you accept your part, circumstances and the outcome may change. Don't wait to resolve it.

CHILDHOOD–MOVE PAST THE BLAME

STRATEGY

You were dealt an unchangeable hand in childhood. You didn't ask for or pick the situations you were placed in but you do have to deal with the outcomes. You have a choice in how you manage them.

You can't let the bad moments define you or the rest of your life. Redefine your present and future by using the not-so-pleasant episodes to redirect what you have learned about them. Start by sharing those experiences with someone you trust.

Life is an ongoing journey with many phases from beginning to end. Childhood is where you start but not where you land. You may not forget where you came from, but you can decide to move past the blame to get to the other side. By letting go of the past, you have room for the future. You didn't get to write the beginning of your story, but you get to participate in writing the rest of the pages.

YOUR NEEDS GO TO THE FRONT OF THE LINE

STRATEGY

Pay attention to and honor what your needs and wants are to live your life. Don't be too willing to sacrifice your own needs ahead of someone else's, unless it is essential. Be willing and able to embrace this mindset and save up your own energy to help others second. Take your needs to the quick checkout lane.

Rule number one: Place your well-being above everything else. This is not being selfish; it's being responsible for your own life. No one will take better care of you than you. No one knows what you want or need better than you. Go live your life and align your hopes and dreams without sacrificing your well-being.

INVEST IN YOURSELF

STRATEGY

You likely make different types of investments, whether they're financial, professional, family, etc. You need to start looking at yourself as the most valuable ROI (return on investment) that you can make. You should spend a significant amount of time and energy focusing on becoming the best representation of yourself. Invest in learning something new or improving your health or your emotional well-being. Make sure you are investing in you!

COURAGE: FIND YOUR VOICE

STRATEGY

If you don't say it, who will? Your best advocate for you is yourself. Be strong; use your voice to communicate and promote your insights and your needs or to stand up to someone being unkind.

Mean what you say and say what you mean. Pull up those adult-size pants, step out of your comfort zone, and set aside your fears and insecurities. You'll never know until you try. Don't wait and hope someone else will say if for you. No one can express what you're thinking or feeling better than you can! Just try—what do you have to lose?

GIVE YOURSELF PERMISSION TO DREAM

STRATEGY

Don't forget to dream from time to time. Give yourself permission and plenty of time to let your mind wonder and imagine the impossible. No matter how out of reach it may seem, you'd be surprised by what is possible. Your mind is the most powerful part of your body—it determines your future.

Begin creating your future—write it down, draw it, record it on your phone, or make a vision board. Whatever your method, save it so you can continually review it and plant the seeds of your dream. Anyone who has created something along the way has had a dream. What's yours?

CONFIDENCE: SAY IT LIKE YOU MEAN IT!

STRATEGY

Be proud of your thoughts and ideas. It takes only one person to say something, so why not you? It doesn't matter if it will have a minor or major impact. Chances are good that you will find another person who supports you and who will walk beside you because they believe in your mission.

Say it like you mean it, even if you're nervous and scared. Say it with force, with conviction in your voice, with a powerful smile and a vote of confidence expelling from your body like you have never felt before.

Own it and present it with the respect it deserves. If you believe it, express it. Don't miss an opportunity because you couldn't find your voice; make your words matter!

DRIVING TOWARD YOUR DESTINY

STRATEGY

Focus on the things you can control and that will bring you closer to your dreams. If you don't have a plan, close your eyes and envision the best possible outcome, then begin to feel it happening. Creating your own destiny starts with taking one step forward. The challenging part is making it attainable with incremental smaller steps and figuring out what's next. Start by creating a process for arriving at your destination. Don't let life happen to you; make life happen for you.

What do you believe is your destiny? Go out and make it happen!

BE YOUR OWN CHEERLEADER

STRATEGY

Pay close attention to your self-talk. If you wouldn't say it to someone else, then don't say it to yourself. Be your own coach and practice positive inner reflection. Be patient and kind during your own dialogue. When you catch yourself thinking negative self-talk, rewind and replay your thoughts with "I can do it" statements. Practice daily. It can be awkward at first but you will see huge benefits.

ENJOY BEING IN YOUR OWN SPACE

STRATEGY

Be sure you carve out time for yourself daily, even if it's only 20 minutes. Ideally, allow or build up to an hour a day. Find the balance between having alone time without feeling lonely and spending time with others. Spend quality time with yourself. It may sound odd at first but you will come to enjoy it.

Remove all distractions. Do one thing you enjoy, such as reading, painting, exercising, taking a bath, or journaling. Whatever it is, enjoy being at peace with yourself. Generate this habit and relish the quiet time. It will bring you to a space to center yourself and allow some peace of mind for you to rejuvenate and rest mentally.

WORK SMARTER AND HARDER ON YOURSELF THAN ANYTHING ELSE

STRATEGY

Dedicate a significant amount of focused time and energy on you and the rest will follow. You can't give your best self if you are depleted. Make the time and take good care of you. This is *your* life. No one else can live it for you. Align your priorities to work toward your goals. If your goal is to save money, for example, then shopping will cause you to be out of alignment with your goal. Also, don't place yourself last. Be first in line to take care of your needs, and then you will be ready to take care of others with more zest in your step.

STRATEGY REINFORCEMENT CHALLENGE #7

One-Degree Shifts Navigate to an Authentic True Self

DAY 1: FOCUS

Focus on bringing more joy to each day. Step one is to list the people or places that keep your spirits up. Step two is to focus on the reasons why they create joy or comfort to you. Write down your initial answers to both but limit it to only five minutes. The goal is to bring your daily focus on joy that is not attached to things.

DAY 2: REMEMBER

Remember to take care of your needs first. Challenge yourself to do at least one thing for yourself today. It could be as simple as reading a book, walking, or hanging out with friends or family. Depleting yourself of joy may bring emptiness. Enjoy your me time. Do something you haven't done in a while—just do it!

DAY 3: PRACTICE

Practice saying "no" in kind ways to honor your own boundaries. You can't be everywhere or do everything. If you need space, take it. Without guilt, take care of your own emotional well-being. You don't owe others an explanation. It's ok to honor yourself first. Incorporate this once a week for life.

INSTRUCTIONS:

Select one challenge per day to observe the full impact. Best practice is to journal the results by the end of each day to fully process the experiences. Pick just one or two or try all three days. The goal is to challenge yourself to do something different in order to grow.

MICROSCOPIC THOUGHTS
SHAPE YOUR ATMOSPHERE

ood things come in teeny-tiny packages. Think about the little moments that build up to your life and the itty-bitty flashes of memories that make up your story. All these moments strung together have brought you to where you are right now.

In this themed section, you will learn an array of universal microscopic thoughts to help you better understand some of the simplest, yet most valuable, life strategies. These are the key strategies that bring it all together to create and build your bliss.

TIME: THE MOST VALUABLE GIFT

STRATEGY

The most precious gift you can give is your time. It's something you just can't buy. Giving time to yourself or someone else should be considered the most valuable investment. Spend your allotment wisely because it goes fast. You can't do it over so make your time count. Time keeps moving forward; it has no pause button and it waits for no one.

Whether you're being super productive or relaxing, enjoy your life. Find your balance with work and play. How you spend your time, who you spend it with, and where you spent it all matters. The entire sum of how you have spent your time equals your life story. Make your time count!

WHEN IN DOUBT, HIT THE RESET BUTTON

STRATEGY

When times get tough and it's not going well—whether it's a conversation, bad decision, job situation, or anything in between—find a way to restart. Remember to find an option to try to stop your part of the circumstances and start with an attempt to *reset* at a point that makes sense. Mistakes are part of life and are the best opportunity for learning. Hit the reset button whenever necessary!

LIFE CAN CHANGE IN AN INSTANT

STRATEGY

Life is full of surprises. New lives begin and sadly, lives end. Any number of circumstances can change in the blink of an eye. Don't take life for granted. If something isn't working in your life, you have the ability to change directions. Life has no guarantees.

A new decision today can bring instant changes for tomorrow. What are you waiting for? Don't wait to change things— do it now!

RIDE THE WAVE OF LIFE

STRATEGY

You will have moments in life when the chaos is all around you but reacting to it may not be helpful. Be strong and ride things out. You do not need to always speak your mind or react in some way; for now, let it be. Allow the opportunity to let things simmer and figure out the lesson to be learned. When you ride the wave, the water eventually comes to shore. Be patient and kind while waiting, for your tide will come in.

ASPIRE TO TRY NEW THINGS

STRATEGY

If you want to feel alive again, try something new, something you haven't done before. Be open and seek out new opportunities, especially if you're feeling stagnate. New experiences can create excitement, take you in new directions, and awaken all your senses.

Even if a new situation brings challenges, you still have a chance to learn from it. You'll learn the most from new things, new people, new places, and new experiences. Be willing to find new ways of doing things. Embrace occasions where life gives you an unexpected circumstance. Even if you feel uncomfortable, work through it. Energize your life with new opportunities!

IT'S ALL IN THE DETAILS

STRATEGY

Take a few minutes to observe where you are right now at this very point in time. Be present in this moment. Take in your environment. Breathe and be aware of all the fine details in your life. Look around your surroundings and notice something new. You may be missing many amazing, significant fine details around you because you're focusing on all the other things. Sometimes it's the smallest details that can give you the biggest inspiration and can guide you. Observe your surroundings; they tell a story. What's your story saying?

YOU HAVE ONLY TWO CHOICES

STRATEGY

When you come to a dilemma, you generally have two choices. You can accept it or not. If you do accept it, be patient and watch things unfold. Be proud of yourself for having the willingness to figure it out.

If you don't accept the situation, what actions are you willing to take to change it? Unwillingness can indicate that it's time to walk away or change course. If you do nothing, you're not really deciding. The decision will be made for you and may not be what you'd pick. Choose what is best for you. You're the only one who can.

LIFE'S CODE: LOOK FOR THE SIGNS

STRATEGY

Life will reveal a secret language to you when you are on the right or wrong path. It shows you a secret code for when you are or are not making the best decisions. If you pay close attention, you'll find subtle signals showing you which path you should be taking. You'll feel it when it's right and when it's not.

Look for the signs that come your way. If things are flowing and moving forward, keep on the current path. If roadblocks appear continually, maybe it's time to change course. Look at what life's code is offering to tell you, then carry on.

APPRECIATE WHAT YOU DO HAVE

STRATEGY

There will always be that next new thing, or new person, or the next new place to go in your life. It's good to want more out of life and strive for bigger and better. The trick is to accept and appreciate what you have right now. Stop to consider what you didn't have a couple years ago. Appreciate and be grateful for what you do have today. This is where true bliss lives. Love what you have and have what you love.

COMPROMISE, COMPROMISE, COMPROMISE

STRATEGY

Find ways to meet others in the middle. Compromise whenever possible and practical. Life is amazing when things are accomplished with others so bring some flexibility to the table. Find the win-win situation and be the solution.

Be the hero! Every team needs one, why not you? Compromise when it makes the most sense without compromising your beliefs. Be reasonable and loveable when sharing thoughts and ideas with others but give others that same opportunity. Be willing to bend a little. Life's better when it's shared.

RECOGNIZE WHEN YOU'RE TRANSITIONING

STRATEGY

You'll continually go through phases in life, especially during different life events or during the aging process. When you hit major life-altering stages or age milestones, you're likely to see and feel differently about yourself. Just before you hit a turning point in your life, your self-perspective may change and make you feel unsettled.

When you approach certain phases, you may begin to feel unprepared. This is very common as you age, as you understand you are about to become a different version of yourself. This could invoke a sense of fear but realize that transitioning is part of the process cycle of life. If you have times when you feel uncomfortable, unsure, or lost, just know you could be in the middle of a transition. Transitioning means you're growing in some way, so embrace it! You have no way around it but going through it.

EMBRACING CHANGE

STRATEGY

Don't be afraid of change. It's likely it is the unknown that you're afraid of, not the change itself, because you don't know yet how it's going to play out. You need to be willing to adapt to life's changes. It may end up being better than you imagined. Be vulnerable to change; ready or not, change will happen. Just go with it and do not hide your head in the sand. You will look back and wonder how you got there.

Change doesn't mean that it's going to be bad. It just means that it's going to be different than before. Embracing change is medicine for the soul.

HAVING A BACKUP PLAN

STRATEGY

If life has taught me nothing else, it has taught me to always have a backup plan. Since change happens so often, and with or without expecting it, life can be very unpredictable. Make sure you have other options in the pipeline for any major decision or plans in order to stay successful in life. This is one of my biggest secrets to navigating life.

Try to be one step ahead of the game, and then you're ready for those curveballs when they're thrown your way. It's great being prepared and organized, just remember to be flexible and compromise when necessary. Having a backup plan is like having alternate directions; in case you come across a road that is closed or has a detour, you'll know right where to go next!

TAKE IT ALL IN CONTEXT

STRATEGY

With all the strategies presented here to help inspire you to balance your life, make sure you use and apply these strategies according to the context of your situation. Be mindful of your intent to be loving and kind. Take good care of yourself and your needs above anything else. Have goals and apply practical decision-making to your life to achieve who you want to be, along with some kind of support. Don't live your life solo—include others. Live your best life, don't just exist. Everything comes to an end sooner or later, so just enjoy the ride during your journey of it all while you can!

CARPE DIEM

STRATEGY

This is one of my favorite inspirational phrases. It gave me momentum during my life's journey when I learned that life is too short. I learned to make better decisions in the moment and when to see that I was on the right path. *Carpe diem* means "seize the day!" Whenever I hear or see this, it immediately gives me an uplifting jolt. It inspires me to give it my all and do the things today that will enrich my life tomorrow.

It also means for you to take a chance and not wait until later. Get out there and live. Do at least one thing that changes your life for the better. Enjoy life now!

STRATEGY REINFORCEMENT CHALLENGE #8

Microscopic Thoughts Shape Your Atmosphere

DAY 1: FOCUS

Focus on the details; you may be missing many details daily. Stop, look, listen, and feel what is around you. Notice something new about someone else, yourself, or your surroundings. Appreciate the little things that you may take for granted. Write down the details you notice today, along with the date. Reflect in 30 days.

DAY 2: REMEMBER

Remember to look for those life codes. The signs can be very subtle or glaring right at you, but simply remember to pay attention to them. Are you on the right path or is something not working? Did you notice any significant signs today? Write them down with the date and how the signs applied to you.

DAY 3: PRACTICE

Practice finding a new opportunity, something that you normally wouldn't do. Record the results. You will learn more about yourself by reaching out of your comfort zone and you'll discover your growth potential. Try one new thing this week and write it down. You may be surprised about what you learn.

INSTRUCTIONS:

Select one challenge per day to observe the full impact. Best practice is to journal the results by the end of each day to fully process the experiences. Pick just one or two or try all three days. The goal is to challenge yourself to do something different in order to grow.

FINAL WISDOM

Write your own script. Life can be difficult, but it also has so many wonderful possibilities. If you need a little help or support to overcome a life hurdle, Phelps Strategies is available. The point is, as a good friend once said to me, "Don't wait and make the world small." In other words, it's your life so make it yours. You get no second chances. Be your best version of you. Above all, try and stay blissful!

Go back and review your journal from the beginning. Notice the dates and situations. Reread it six months from now. It's funny how much changes in such a short time and what you may have thought was important really wasn't.

For additional information, please visit our website at www.phelpsconsulting.net.

Made in the USA
Coppell, TX
05 January 2021